Everyday Prayers for Men

EVERYDAY PRAYERS
for
Men

DIMENSIONS
FOR LIVING

NASHVILLE

EVERYDAY PRAYERS FOR MEN

95 96 97 98 99 00 01 02 — 10 9 8 7 6 5 4

This book is printed on recycled, acid-free paper.

ISBN 0-687-31691-X

The Steps of Prayer is adapted from HOW TO PRAY,
E. Stanley Jones. Copyright © 1943 by Whitmore and
Stone.

Prayers on pages 43–56 are adapted from *Blessings for
Church Occasions* by Ruth C. Ikerman. Copyright © 1987
by Abingdon Press. Used by permission.

Contents

The Steps of Prayer

First, decide what you really want. The "you" is important. It must not be a vagrant part of you wandering into the prayer hour with no intention of committing yourself to your prayer request. You cannot pray with a part of yourself and expect God to answer, for God hears what the whole of you is saying . . .

Second, decide whether the thing you want is a Christian thing. God has shown us in Christ what the divine character is like. God is Christ-like. He can only act in a Christ-like way. He cannot answer a prayer that would not fit in with his character . . .

Third, write it down. The writing of the prayer will probably help you in self-committal. For, if you write it, you will probably mean it. The writing of it will also save you from hazy indefiniteness. . . . There will come a time, of course, when you may not need to write things down, for they will have written themselves in you . . .

Fourth, still the mind. The stilling of the mind is a step in receptivity. Prayer is pure receptivity in the first stage. "As many as received him, to them gave he power." If you come to God all tense, you can get little . . .

Now you are ready for the fifth step: Talk with God about it. "Talk with God," not "Talk to God," for it is a two-way conversation. And the most vital part may be, not what you will say to God, but what God will say to you . . .

There is a sixth step: . . . at this point be silent to hear God again, and see if he makes any suggestions to you about your part in answering the prayer. If definite suggestions come to you, then promise that you will carry them out . . .

Seventh: Do everything loving that comes to your mind about it! This step is important, for it is a cleansing and clarifying step. The word "loving" is important. The first fruit of the Spirit is "love," and if the suggestion does not fit in with love then don't do it.

Wait for the suggestion that does fit in.

Eighth: thank God for answering in his own way. God will answer that prayer. No prayers are unanswered. But God may answer "no" as well as "yes." "No" is an answer, and it may really be next in order leading on to a higher "yes."

There is a ninth step: Release the whole prayer from your conscious thinking. Don't keep the prayer at the center of your conscious thinking. It may become an anxiety-center. Let it drop down into the sub-conscious mind and let it work at that greater depth. Then there will be an undertone of prayer in all you do, but there will be no tense anxiety. Dismissing it from the conscious mind is an act of faith that, having committed it to God you leave it in his hands, believing he will do the best thing possible . . .

E. Stanley Jones

Before a Day's Work

Dear God I pray that as I go to work today, that I will be able to act upon the things I know to be true:

That my task belongs to me and must be done by me with no expectation that others should do it.

Help me to be responsible.

That my work partners need my support and encouragement for their tasks.

Help me to give to others.

That my employer deserves good quality performance from me.

Help me to do my very best.

That those persons who come to my employer for goods and services must be given good value in exchange for their payment.

Help me to provide good value.

That I should demonstrate that you, dear God, are my greatest motivator for success.

Help me to show your presence within me.

Dear God, I pray that as I go to work today I will be able to act upon the things I know to be true. AMEN.

Thanks for a Day Alone

Creator God, life is made more interesting by the pace of traffic on the road, the crowd of people in the stores, the noise of radio and TV, the press of hand shaking and hugging at church, the call of "Daddy" and "Honey" from children and wife. I don't forget that these are all part of your creation, and I am not ungrateful.

Still, silence and solitude are precious to me. Whether I am physically apart from the hubbub or crave a place of aloneness out of the din with my focused attention, I have freedom.

I am free to dispassionately contemplate whatever things I want to. Free to spend all my emotion on the things I care about most. Free to pretend I'm somebody else in another time. Free to open myself fully to my God.

Thank you, Creator God, for making both the roar of culture and a way and a place for escaping it. Your thoughtfulness in creation is complete. Praise to you. AMEN.

For My Wife

I wish I was a perfect husband. I pray to be much better than I am. Sometimes I sit and look at my wife and am filled with amazement that she has chosen to be my companion, my partner, my lover. My head and heart are filled with the memories of all our best moments—my hard times at work when she has been my comforter and supporter, my times of self-doubt when she has been my encourager, our times of play, our times of lovemaking. I am so grateful for her.

But there are other times when I am not so grateful. This woman who shares a home with me fails to understand my every mood, disagrees with me on what car to buy, gets angry when I'm not home when I say I will be, and seems to always know better than I do how to talk to my own mother. I am so frustrated by her.

Father, help me to see my wife with just the right balance of love, friendship, devotion, respect, joy, gratitude, and clarity.

Help me to be all the things she needs me to be—loving, honest, dependable, sensible, and supporting.

I will try Lord; I will try to be a better husband. Help me. AMEN.

For a Friend Upon Retirement

Father, please stand by my friend
(name) who is nearing retirement.

Some days, he is filled with doubt and
wonders how he will ever fill his time, how
he will be happy without a career, how he
will deal with solitude, how he will handle
more time with his wife, if he will find any
new interests, if he will live long or quickly
die of boredom and inaction.

Other days, he is emotionally sailing,
dreaming of the days when he will be finished with the tension of work, when he
will finally have time to enjoy his wife's
company, when he will be able to finish
painting the house and begin a new
hobby!

He is driving himself crazy alternating
positive and negative moods about retirement. Help me to be a rock of stability in
his life of change. Help me to say the right

things just when he needs to hear them. Help him to see that retirement will be both insecurity and strength, but more than either of these will be a time to continuity. He will still have his wife, his friends, his home, his interests, his talents, and his God.

Thank you, God, for your steadiness in his life. AMEN.

When I Have Not Been Honest

Father, God, I meant to talk to you about the lie I told this morning. I meant to confess my sin and ask for forgiveness.

But suddenly I realized that talking only about this morning's sin would be dishonest with you. How I wish that today's lie was the only untruthfulness I have ever committed.

In fact, I have not admitted to or asked forgiveness for many things—the little lie of last week, the omission I made in an excuse to my friend, all the times I ever said I couldn't when the truth was I wouldn't, and the dozens of other transgressions great and small.

Please, Lord, hear this confession of dishonesty and forgive me.

Please, Lord, hear this confession of attempting to hide sins from you and forgive me. AMEN.

When Success Comes

Lord, I dreamed and planned that my efforts would lead to this success that has come to me. I feel good that I have done well and that others acknowledge my good work and success.

Now, Lord, help me, in the face of success, to push away vanity. Thank you for filling me with the realization that all talents exhibited were gifts from you. Thank you for reminding me that skills I used to achieve this success were aided by parents, teachers, and associates who have spent time and effort with me.

Thank you for helping me reorder my view of my place in the world. Success comes not from the individual alone, but from the support of many.

With gratitude, AMEN.

For Thinking of Others First

Dear Lord, as I begin this new day, I am thankful for the opportunity to share your loving-kindness with others. So often I am preoccupied with my own concerns and needs that I forget to reach out in love to others—to strangers, co-workers, neighbors, and sometimes even my own family. Today I pray for humility and sympathy. Give me the sensitivity to recognize the hurts of those whose paths I cross today, and use me to minister to those hurts in whatever way I can. Replace my selfish thoughts with compassionate thoughts of others. Help me to remember that, as I put others before myself, I receive so much more than I give. AMEN.

Christmas Prayer

Father, as a man I am struck by the man's story in the nativity. Joseph is told he will be a stepfather. Is he supposed to be happy about this? We men always want to control the important decisions in our lives. Still, this stepchild was the Messiah. Help me, like Joseph, to accept responsibility in my life.

Joseph was forced into a stable with his wife, at the very time she was to give birth. How frustrated he must have been to be unable to provide a suitable place for his family. We men want always to have our pride in providing for our families. Still, God did not reject the manger for his son. Help me like Joseph to accept the help of others.

Joseph witnessed a parade of visitors who came to worship the child. No one noticed him or congratulated him. Was he just a little jealous? We men like to be the center of attention. Still, this babe was the center of history. Help me, like Joseph, to take my right place.

Oh, God, thank you for bringing Joseph this simple, accepting man, to be my model. And thank you for my personal savior—Jesus, the Babe of long ago and the Master of today. AMEN.

Easter Prayer

Alleluia, He is Risen, Alleluia! I ask for nothing this day, dear God. For the Lord is risen. He was dead, but now he lives. My Savior lives.

The world was in mourning, but now all creation sings. I need nothing more this day, Dear God. Alleluia, He is Risen, Alleluia!

Feeling Sorry for Myself

Remember, Lord, when I was younger and first discovered I am not the center of creation? I had such big plans for that day. But from the very beginning nothing seemed to go right. The day was a complete disaster, made even worse when someone close to me told me to quit whining. Did I think I could have whatever I wanted just by wishing it?

Remember the angry prayer I began? I stormed about the injustice of my failed expectations, the unfairness of my friends and family, the constant level of disappointment, and the sorrow of being ignored by you.

That was also the first time I felt like I really got an answer in prayer. Very gently, but very insistently, you agreed with my friends. You comforted me, and slowly I became calm. I promised to never again think of myself as the most important part of creation.

But I have not kept that promise. Today I am immersed in self-pity and I need to have your gentle guidance once more. Lead me to quiet acceptance, oh God; I am yours. AMEN.

For My Pastor's Family

Almighty God, families are a special blessing. Today I thank you for the members of our pastor's family. They enrich so many lives in so many ways. Too often I forget to tell them how important they are to me and how much I appreciate their gifts of time, sacrifice, and service. Help me to find the right times and the right ways to show my appreciation and love for them. And help me to remember to tell others of this appreciation, so that they may be reminded to share their love as well. The expectations and demands on the pastor's family are great, and I pray that you will strengthen and sustain them through the difficult times. Pour out your blessings upon their home, and enable them to find time to nurture their family relationships and simply enjoy being together. In Jesus' name I pray. AMEN.

For Adventure in Everyday Living

O God, sometimes my days seem so dull and dreary. I fall into a rut, and I don't know how to climb out. Then, when I think I've found a way out, a way to infuse my life with excitement and renewed energy, I allow my fear of change to overcome me. Help me to break out of the endless cycle of routine and predictability. Give me the courage and the faith to make each day an adventure, trusting in your steadfast love and protection. As I seek your guidance through prayer and meditation upon your word, I ask for the wisdom to make constructive changes in my life and to find new meaning and pleasure in the familiar. Knowing that you walk with me, I can face each new day with joyful anticipation. Thank you for your precious gift of life. AMEN.

A Vacation Prayer

Dear Lord, how I've waited for this vacation, and now it's finally here. Thank you, Lord, for the opportunity to take a break from my daily routine and to replenish my mind, body, and soul so that I may better serve you. Sometimes my expectations for vacations are unrealistic, and I find myself disappointed when things don't go my way. Help me not to worry about having the "perfect" vacation but to relax and enjoy every moment, whatever it may bring. I am grateful for the joys that await me—whether they be the beauty of your creation, recreation with family or friends, or peace and solitude. Watch over me and protect me as I travel, and bring me safely home again—refreshed and renewed. AMEN.

Change in Life-style

Dear Lord, I see friends and acquaintances having to make changes in their life through no fault of their own: The husband who suddenly lost his wife of more than forty years. The wife who lost her husband to cancer after suffering a long illness. The young wife and mother who lost her husband when he was shot by an irate tenant. The young boy who was disfigured for life by burns he sustained in a fire. The elderly who have lost their health and must be placed in a nursing home away from family and friends. I pray that your loving spirit will be with each of them as they enter into a life different from what they have known. Give them your grace and love. Comfort and sustain them when they feel all hope is lost. Lead and guide them when they feel so alone. Make me mindful of their special needs and give me the grace to show care and understanding.

As our lives intertwine, show me how to give light to hopeless darkness, peace where there is turmoil, joy where there is sadness, and sympathy where there is sorrow. I ask this in the name of Jesus Christ, your son. AMEN.

A Morning Prayer

Thank you, dear God, for the peaceful rest of the night and for this glorious morning. May I see everything in this new day as if I had been born anew. Let yesterday's worries and annoyances stay there. Through all the hours of this day, may I walk in the way of love. As I speak with others may I bring a lift to their spirits. Enable me to do my work well, to think on the things that enrich the spirit. I pray that this will be a day of accomplishment and that your joy will be continually in my heart. AMEN.

For a Fruitful Prayer Life

Father, I come asking for help in my prayer life. Too often in the past my prayers have been only a form to be finished quickly so that I might get on to what I found more interesting. But I want my prayers to be more important than anything else. I want to make them so real and so vital that I can truly reach you and find strength and help for all areas of my life. Fill me with your spirit and make me sincere and true in every way. AMEN.

To Be Thankful

Each day I see before me, Lord God,
good reason for thanksgiving. Thank you
for helping me find the happiness of quiet,
simple things; for the contentment that
comes from looking at a pot of flowers on a
window ledge, at the light of an open fire
on the hearth, or at color splashed across
the evening sky. I pray for happiness and
harmony within my home and with everyone I meet today. I pray for the happiness
of being as nearly as I can at all times honest and sincere. I pray for the inner joy
that Jesus knew. In his name. AMEN.

Real Values

Father, I thank you for simple things—for bread and water, for fresh air, and for friendly smiles. Keep me from placing too much value in my possessions. Help me realize that the only real values are within me. Teach me to use my thoughts wisely and well. Remind me that what I am is more important than what I have. Forgive me for proudly parading my possessions before others. Keep me humble and helpful, asking little, giving much. In Jesus' name. AMEN.

For Disappointment

Lord, I've had such a disappointment today. Something I had hoped for, dreamed of, and yes, even prayed for is just not to be. I'm hurt and I'm angry. Help me to turn loose of this bitterness. Now I see only darkness and despair. Light your lamp within me, O Lord of Light. May I see clearly through this shadow that has fallen across my life. Remind me that just as the darkness of night only hides the day for a few hours, your light shines on behind the darkness of my difficulties and disappointments. AMEN.

To Be Worthy

Dear Lord, I turn away from you even when I know better. Forgive me again and again. Help me in the same way to forgive those who are disloyal to me. Build into my character a steady, unfailing spirit of goodwill toward everyone that cannot be influenced by anything that may be done to me. Make me your worthy child. AMEN.

For Carrying on Christ's Work

O, Christ of the loving heart, who felt tenderness and compassion for all people, inspire me to feel the same, I pray. I do not have your power to heal and restore, but your Spirit lives within me. Smile through my face, speak through my voice, use me to help the sick and suffering, the discouraged and lonely. I want to carry on your work. AMEN.

For Giving God First Place

Dear God, when I am troubled or in trouble I come to you pleading for your help, but too often when things are going well I forget about you. Help me to see your loving guidance all the time—every hour, every day. Help me to stay close to you in prosperity and success just as in difficulty and failure. Help me to put you first in my life and to hold to that standard always. AMEN.

For God's Help in Relationships

All wise and loving God, you know how blind I can be to my own faults and how quick I sometimes am to see the faults of others. Clear my eyes, I pray, so that I can see both myself and others as we truly are. Help me to practice your great commandments to love you with all my being and to love others as myself. I can't do it alone, but with your help I can. Thank you for your unfailing love. AMEN.

A Christmas Shopping Prayer

O Christ Jesus whose birth so long ago began the traditions of today, thank you for the privilege of Christmas shopping. Help me to make even what could be a stress-filled time a time of wonder and excitement. Let me look at the Christmas decorations on city streets with the eyes of a child, to hear beyond the tinny sounds of recorded music the words of the story of your great gift to us. Make me patient in crowds, quick to smile and in some way bring a lift to the spirits of those whose work is heavier at this time. May each gift be chosen in your name and may I always give with love. AMEN.

With God

Begin the day with God:
Kneel down and say a prayer;
Lift up your heart to God's abode
And seek God's love to share.

Go through the day with God,
Whate'er your work may be;
Where'er you are—at home, abroad,
God still is near to thee.

Conclude the day with God:
Your sins to God confess;
Trust in the Lord's atoning blood,
And plead God's righteousness.

Author Unknown (adapted)

The Meaning of Prayer

A breath of prayer in the morning
Means a day of blessing sure—
A breath of prayer in the evening
Means a night of rest secure.

A breath of prayer in our weakness
Means the clasp of a mighty hand—
A breath of prayer when we're lonely
Means someone to understand.

A breath of prayer in rejoicing
Gives joy and added delight.
For they that remember God's goodness
Go singing far into the night.

There's never a year nor a season
That prayer may not bless every hour
And never a soul need be helpless
When linked with God's great power.

Author Unknown

Blessing for an Annual Church Dinner

Our dear loving heavenly Father, we are grateful for this opportunity of Christian fellowship with one another and with you. Please be very near this night to our dear shut-ins who are not able to meet with us physically, but whose hearts join with ours in hope and love for this church. We remember with warm hearts also the women and men who have shared our spiritual dreams and who are now gone from this earthly life.

We ask you to give us an abiding sense of your own continuous presence in times of change. May we each take from the past the blessing of joyous memories, and grant that the inspiration of this gathering may give us fresh energy for future activities in your kingdom.

Bless this food to our bodies and this fellowship to our hearts that we may serve you better in our homes, through this church, and in our community and nation. These mercies we ask in the precious name of your son, Jesus, our Lord and our Savior. AMEN.

Blessing for a Stewardship Meeting

Dear God, we would be willing stewards of your bounty, ever grateful for the abundance of goodness with which you fill our hearts. We are aware of the great gifts of health and energy to work day by day and for the natural blessings of earth, air, and water. Forgive us for the times we have taken these elements for granted, forgetting that you are the giver of every good and perfect gift.

Now as we come together to consider our stewardship of such gifts, place in our hearts generous motives of unselfish giving as reflections of your wondrous gifts to us. Grant us wisdom to know how best to share our financial blessings with other persons that they may be encouraged to live Christian lives and, in turn, may be enabled to bless others and to serve you better.

From this discussion, may we all come away with renewed appreciation of our daily blessings and fresh strength to find Christian solutions to today's problems. AMEN.

Blessing for a Choir Supper

Kind Lord, precious Lord, be very near to us as we gather in happy fellowship with choir members of our own church. Let harmony reign in all our hearts as together we partake of these blessings of food and conversation.

We thank you for the opportunities we have to carol your praises in weekly services, leading others to know the beauty and power of the precious heritage of church music. Let us always be aware of music as a ministry for present needs. May our music be extended into the lives of those who listen, that they may be encouraged when discouraged, strengthened when weak, and always enabled to face life anew with a song in their hearts.

Keep our voices and our lives in harmony with your will. AMEN.

Blessing for a Monthly Group Meeting

Dear Father, as the time for our monthly meeting arrives, we are aware of how quickly the days and weeks speed past. We are grateful that we can meet today with our common interest in mind. Help us to make wise use of the time allotted for consideration of our business that your kingdom may be advanced by our activities in this area. Undergird our deliberations with a spirit of unity and with a deep desire to serve you better everyday. Grant each heart here a blessing to carry home to enrich the days of work and play until we meet again. May each month find us further along on our journey of faith. In Jesus' name, AMEN.

Prayer for a Bible Study Class

Dear God, we thank you for this opportunity to learn about the Bible with the help of our fine teacher. Show us how to make the most of the time we spend together so that we may gain information and inspiration to live our lives better. We are grateful to be able to spend time with friends in this class and to have a chance to make new ones. Bless this class and our church. We ask this in Jesus' name. AMEN.

Prayer for an Outdoor Worship Service

God of the open air, we come to you grateful for the outdoors and all that it offers in the way of recreation and pleasure for all ages. We thank you also for our church, with its regular routine, and the members with whom we may share this informal outdoor fellowship.

Help us all to relax and know that we are indeed your children, welcome in all your world to enjoy the beauty of mountains, seashore, desert, trees, and flowers. In this relaxed setting, may our minds be free from trivia and clutter, so that we may see clearly our opportunities to serve you better. Grant us fresh energy and renewed zest to serve you better. Bless each of us and our church so that we may reach others for you. AMEN.

Blessing for Graduation Recognition

Dear Father, we come to this milestone in the lives of students with deep gratitude for the teachings of eternal truths in the Bible. We are grateful for this opportunity of fellowship that celebrates the achievements of the mind in learning about your wonderful world. We remember with appreciation all the parents who were the first teachers of these students, even before they met their first school teachers. And we would not forget the dedicated Sunday school teachers who in their limited weekly times have taught the rules of Christian behavior. Grant that from this happy occasion we may all draw fresh strength for further study in our homes and churches. AMEN.

Prayer for a Church Retreat

Father of us all, be very near to this group as our church family gathers for a retreat to renew our spiritual strength and to plan ahead for future growth. We would not walk before you, but ask you to lead us in all our discussions and in facing up to the problems and demands of the present age.

We are grateful for this opportunity to meet together away from the daily responsibilities of routine. Grant that from this fellowship may come new friendships and a heightened sense of our togetherness as Christians united in a common cause.

Let there be moments of lighthearted play and pleasure to balance our serious discussions and our planning for future events. May this be a time of strengthened spiritual resolve to live daily lives that testify to your power and saving grace. AMEN.

Prayer for a Church Anniversary

O gracious Lord, we give you thanks for the great blessing of your loving presence with our church across the changing years of Christian service. We are grateful for those founding members who cared enough about the verities of eternity to found this church in a first building of worship. We remember the later sacrifices of time and talent so that more adequate facilities could be provided for their children and grandchildren to learn about God and how to live as Christians. Today we ask anew for a special portion of your power that we may never become indifferent to the values of Christian fellowship, with one another and with the other churches in our beloved community. Even as we celebrate our commitment, help us to realize with humility our human frailties and to remember your promise that a thousand years with you are as but a day. Let our day be strengthened with the righteousness that comes from you. These mercies we ask in the name of your Son, Jesus, our Lord and our Savior. AMEN.

A Prayer for the New Year

Dear God, our minds and hearts turn in two directions as we recall the many blessings of the past year and look ahead to anticipated blessings of the year just beginning. None of us can know what of joy or sorrow will come into our lives, but we are grateful for the reassurance that you will be with us whatever situations we face.

Hear our thanks for the lasting joys of precious memories that keep the past a part of the present. Help us so to live day by day that we may build new memories to bless the future with happiness. Let no opportunity for service escape our knowledge, as with eyes of love we survey our surroundings and the needs of our loved one.

May this be a year in which our hearts are enlarged to embrace those who need assurance of your love. AMEN.

A Benediction

Dear God, our hearts are filled with thanks for the joy and blessing of fellowship with great minds and spirits through personal contacts, letters, books, music, travel, and all the many opportunities afforded by our church. Forgive us the times we have failed to take advantage of what is available to us in our weekly Sunday services and various midweek events. Accept our thanks for the rewarding satisfaction of achievements, whether at small tasks or large. Above all, hear our gratitude for a growing knowledge for you through the spiritual influence of church activities. Grant to each heart the blessing of your enduring peace, that our lives may be a benediction of blessing to others. AMEN.

Christian Prayers Through the Centuries

For Joy and Gladness

Blessed are Thou, O Lord, who has nourished me from my youth up, who givest food to all flesh. Fill our hearts with joy and gladness that we, always having all sufficiency in all things, may abound to every good work in Christ Jesus our Lord, through whom to Thee be glory, honor, might, majesty and dominion, forever and ever. AMEN.

The Clementine Liturgy
First Century

For Stewardship

O Lord God Almighty, who has built
Thy Church upon the foundation of the
Apostles, under Christ the head corner-
stone, and to this end didst endue Thy
holy apostle St. Barnabas with the singular
gift of the Holy Ghost; leave me not desti-
tute, I humbly beseech Thee, of Thy mani-
fold gifts and talents, nor yet of grace to
make a right use of them always without
any sordid self-ends, to Thy honour and
glory; that, making a due improvement of
all those gifts Thou graciously entrustest
me with, I may be able to give a good
account of my stewardship when the great
Judge shall appear, the Lord Jesus Christ,
who reigneth with Thee and the Eternal
Spirit, one God, blessed forever. AMEN.

Barnabas
Second Century

Prayer for God's Help

Give perfection to beginners, O Father;
give intelligence to the little ones; give aid
to those who are running their course.
Give sorrow to the negligent; give fervor
to spirit to the lukewarm. Give to the perfect a good consummation; for the sake of
Christ Jesus our Lord. AMEN.

Irenaeus
Second Century

Christ, Be with Me

Christ, be with me, Christ before me,
Christ behind me,
Christ in me, Christ beneath me, Christ
above me,
Christ on my right, Christ on my left.
Christ when I lie, Christ when I sit, Christ
when I arise,
Christ in the heart of every one who
thinks of me,
Christ in the mouth of every one who
speaks of me,
Christ in every eye that sees me.
Christ in every ear that hears me.
 Salvation is of the Lord,
 Salvation is of the Lord,
 Salvation is of the Christ,
 May your salvation, O Lord, be ever
 with us.

St. Patrick
Fifth Century

Daily Prayer of Thomas Aquinas

Grant me, I beseech Thee, O merciful God, prudently to study, rightly to understand, and perfectly to fulfill that which is pleasing to Thee, to the praise and glory of Thy name.

Thou, O Christ, art the King of glory; Thou art the everlasting Son of the Father. AMEN.

Thomas Aquinas
Thirteenth Century

Praising God of Many Names

O burning Mountain, O chosen Sun,
O perfect Moon, O fathomless Well,
O unattainable Height, O Clearness
    beyond Measure,
O Wisdom without end, O Mercy without
    limit,
O Strength beyond resistance, O Crown
    beyond all majesty:
The humblest thing you created sings your
    praise. AMEN.

Mechtil of Magdelburg
Germany, *Thirteenth Century*

For Thy Spirit

The prayers I make will then be sweet
   indeed,
If Thou the spirit give by which I pray;
My unassisted heart is barren clay,
That of its native self can nothing feed;
Of good and pious works Thou art the seed
That quickens only where Thou say'st it may.
Unless Thou show to us Thy own true way,
No man can find it! Father! Thou must lead;
Do Thou then breathe those thoughts into
   my mind
By which such virtue may in me be bred
That in Thy holy footsteps I may tread;
The fetters of my tongue do Thou unbind,
That I may have the power to sing to Thee,
And sound Thy praises everlastingly!
   AMEN.

Michelangelo
Fifteenth Century

Prayer for Friends

Almighty, everlasting God, have mercy on Thy servants our friends. Keep them continually under Thy protection, and direct them according to Thy gracious favour in the way of everlasting salvation; that they may desire such things as please Thee, and with all their strength perform the same. And forasmuch as they trust in Thy mercy, vouchsafe, O Lord, graciously to assist them with Thy heavenly help, that they may ever diligently serve Thee, and by no temptations be separated from Thee; through Jesus Christ our Lord. AMEN.

Thomas à Kempis
Fifteenth Century

Prayer for Consolation and Support

O Thou most sweet and loving Lord, Thou knowest mine infirmities, and the necessities which I endure; in how great evils and sins I am involved; how often I am weighed down, tempted, and disturbed by them. I entreat of Thee consolation and support. I speak to Thee who knowest all things, to whom all my inward thoughts are open, and who alone canst perfectly comfort and help me. Thou knowest what things I stand in most need of. Behold, I stand before Thee poor and naked, calling for grace, and imploring mercy. Refresh Thy hungry supplicant, kindle my coldness with the fire of Thy love, enlighten my blindness with the brightness of Thy presence. Suffer me not to go away from Thee hungry and dry, but deal mercifully with

me, as often times Thou has dealt wonder-
fully with Thy saints. AMEN.

Thomas à Kempis

The Sufficiency of God

God, of your goodness give me yourself;
for you are sufficient for me. I cannot prop-
erly ask anything less, to be worthy of you.
If I were to ask less I should always be in
want. In you alone do I have all. AMEN.

Julian of Norwich
Fifteenth Century

Give Me Grace

Give me thy grace, good Lord,
To set the world at nought,
To set my mind fast on thee.
And not to hang upon the blast of men's
    mouths.
To be content to be solitary,
Not to long for world company,
Little and little utterly to cast off the
    world,
And rid my mind of all the business
    thereof.
Gladly to be thinking of God,
Piteously to call for his help,
To lean upon the comfort of God,
Busily to labor to love him.

Thomas More
Sixteenth Century

Teach Me to Be Generous

Dearest Lord, teach me to be generous;
Teach me to serve thee as thou deservest;
To give and not to count the cost,
To fight and not to heed the wounds,
To toil and not to seek for rest,
To labour and not to seek reward,
Save that of knowing that I do thy will.

Ignatius of Loyola
Sixteenth Century

Morning Prayer

We give thanks unto thee, heavenly Father, through Jesus Christ thy dear Son, that thou hast protected us through the night from all danger and harm; and we beseech thee to preserve and keep us, this day also, from all sin and evil; that in all our thoughts, words, and deeds, we may serve and please thee. Into thy hands we command our bodies and souls, and all that is ours. Let thy holy angel have charge concerning us that the wicked one have no power over us. AMEN.

Martin Luther
Sixteenth Century

For Peace

In these our days so perilous,
Lord, peace in mercy send us;
No God but thee can fight for us,
No God but thee defend us;
  Thou our only God and Savior.

Martin Luther
Sixteenth Century

For Imitation of Christ

Almighty God, inasmuch as thou hast been pleased to set before us an example of every perfection in thine only-begotten Son, grant that we may study to form ourselves in imitation of him. May we follow not only what he has prescribed, but also what he performed, that we may truly prove ourselves to be his members, and thus confirm our adoption. May we so proceed in the whole course of our life that we may at length be gathered into that blessed rest which the same, thine only-begotten Son, hath obtained for us by his own blood. AMEN.

John Calvin
Sixteenth Century

Reliance on God

O Lord,
never suffer us to think
that we can stand by ourselves,
and not need thee.

John Donne
Seventeenth Century

Fix Then Our Steps

Fix Thou our steps, O Lord, that we stagger not at the uneven motions of the world, but steadily go on to our glorious home, neither censuring our journey by the weather we meet with, nor turning out of the way for anything that befalls us.

John Wesley
Eighteenth Century

For Holiness

Cure us, O thou great Physician of souls, of all our sinful distempers.

Cure us of this intermitting piety, and fix it into an even and a constant holiness.

Oh, make us use religion as our regular diet and not only as a medicine in necessity.

Make us enter into a course of hearty repentance and practice virtue as our daily exercise.

So shall our souls be endued with perfect health and disposed for a long, even for an everlasting, life.

John Wesley

Jesus, Lover of My Soul

Jesus, lover of my soul,
Let me to thy bosom fly,
While the nearer waters roll,
While the tempest still is high:
Hide me, O my Savior, hide,
Till the storm of life is past;
Safe into the haven guide;
O receive my soul at last!

Charles Wesley
Eighteenth Century

Prayer

Only, O Lord, in Thy dear love
Fit us for perfect rest above:
And help us this and every day,
To live more nearly as we pray.

John Keble
Nineteenth Century

For Peace

O Lord, support us all the day long of
this troublous life, until the shadows
lengthen, and the evening comes, and the
busy world is hushed, and the fever of life
is over, and our work is done. Then, in
Thy great mercy, grant us a safe lodging,
and a holy rest, and peace at the last;
through Jesus Christ our Lord. AMEN.

John Henry Newman
Nineteenth Century

Stay With Me

Stay with me, and then I shall begin to shine as thou shinest: so to shine as to be a light to others. The light, O Jesus, will be all from thee. None of it will be mine. No merit to me. It will be thou who shinest through me upon others. O let me thus praise thee, in the way which thou dost love best, by shining on all those around me. Give light to them as well as to me; light them with me, through me. Teach me to show forth thy praise, thy truth, thy will. Make me preach thee without preaching—not by words, but by my example and by the catching force, the sympathetic influence, of what I do—by my visible resemblance to thy saints, and the evident fulness of the love which my heart bears to thee.

John Henry Newman

Ever a Child

Thou, O my God, art ever new, though thou art the most ancient—thou alone art the floor for eternity. I am to live for ever, not for a time—and I have no power over my being; I cannot destroy myself, even though I were so wicked as to wish to do so. I must live on, with intellect and consciousness for ever, in spite of myself. Without thee eternity would be another name for eternal misery. In thee alone have I that which can stay me up for ever: thou alone art the food of my soul. Thou alone art inexhaustible, and ever offerest to me something new to know, something new to love . . . and so on for eternity I shall ever be a little child beginning to be taught the rudiments of thy infinite divine nature. For thou art thyself the seat and centre of all good, and the only substance in this universe of shadows, and the heaven in which blessed spirits live and rejoice—AMEN.

John Henry Newman

To the Holy Spirit

As the wind is thy symbol
so forward our goings.
As the dove
so launch us heavenwards.
As water
so purify our spirits.
As a cloud
so abate our temptations.
As dew
so revive our languor.
As fire
so purge out our dross.

Christina Rossetti
Nineteenth Century

For Illumination

Open wide the window of our spirits, O
Lord, and fill us full of light; open wide the
door of our hearts, that we may receive
and entertain thee with all our powers of
adoration and love. AMEN.

Christina Rossetti
Nineteenth Century

Thy Greatness

God in Heaven, let me really feel my
nothingness, not in order to despair over
it, but in order to feel the more powerfully
the greatness of Thy goodness.

Søren Kierkegaard
Nineteenth Century

Thou Hast Loved Us First

Father in Heaven! Thou hast loved us first, help us never to forget that Thou art love so that this sure conviction might triumph in our hearts over the seduction of the world, over the inquietude of the soul, over the anxiety for the future, over the fright of the past, over the distress of the moment. But grant also that this conviction might discipline our soul so that our heart might remain faithful and sincere in the love which we bear to all those whom Thou hast commanded us to love as we love ourselves.

Søren Kierkegaard
Nineteenth Century

Waking

Father in Heaven! When the thought of Thee wakes in our hearts let it not awaken like a frightened bird that flies about in dismay, but like a child waking from its sleep with a heavenly smile.

Søren Kierkegaard
Nineteenth Century

My Heart

Father, into thy hands I give the heart
Which left thee but to learn how good
thou art.

George Macdonald
Twentieth Century

A Fool I Bring

When I look back upon my life nigh spent,
Nigh spent, although the stream as yet
  flows on,
I more of follies than of sins repent,
Less for offence than love's shortcomings
  moan.
With self, O Father, leave me not alone—
Leave not with the beguiler the beguiled;
Besmirched and ragged, Lord, take back
  thine own;
A fool I bring thee to be made a child.

George Macdonald

In Praise of the Night

O Lord, we praise Thee for our sister, the
Night, who folds all the tired folk of the
earth in her comfortable robe of darkness
and give them sleep. Release now the
strained limbs of toil and smooth the brow
of care. Grant us the refreshing draught of
forgetfulness, that we may rise in the morning with a smile on our face. Comfort and
ease those who toss wakeful on a bed of
pain, or those whose aching nerves crave
sleep and find it not. Save them from evil or
despondent thoughts in the long darkness,
and teach them so to lean on Thy all-per-
vading life and love, that their souls may
grow tranquil and their bodies, too, may rest.
And now, through Thee we send Good
Night to all our brothers and sisters near and
far, and pray for peace upon all the earth.
AMEN.

Walter Rauschenbusch

For the Spirit of Truth

From the cowardice that dares not face
    new truth,
from the laziness that is contented with
    half-truth,
from the arrogance that thinks it knows all
    truth,
Good Lord, deliver me. AMEN.

Prayer from Kenya

A Refuge Amid Distraction

Like an ant on a stick both ends of which
are burning,
    I go to and fro without knowing what
        to do,
      and in great despair.
Like the inescapable shadow that
     follows me,
   the dead weight of sin haunts me.
Graciously look upon me.
Thy love is my refuge. AMEN.

Traditional
India

For the Unity of Christ's Body

Help each of us, gracious God,
   to live in such magnanimity and restraint
that the Head of the church may never have
cause to say to any one of us,
   "This is my body, broken by you." AMEN.

Chinese Prayer

For a New Day

We give you hearty thanks for the rest of
   the past night
     and for the gift of a new day, with its
      opportunities of pleasing you.
Grant that we may so pass its hours in the
   perfect freedom of your service,
   that at eventide we may again give
     thanks unto you. AMEN.

Eastern Orthodox Prayer

For Protection at Night

Dear Jesus, as a hen covers her chicks with her wings to keep them safe, do thou this night protect us under your golden wings. AMEN.

Traditional
India

For a Peaceful Night

O God, you have let me pass the day in
   peace;
let me pass the night in peace, O Lord who
   has no Lord.
There is no strength but in you. You alone
   have no obligation.
Under your hand I pass the night.
You are my Mother and my Father. AMEN.

Traditional prayer of the Boran people

For True Life

Govern all by thy wisdom, O Lord,
   so that my soul may always be serving
      thee
         as thou dost will,
         and not as I may choose.
Do not punish me, I beseech thee,
   by granting that which I wish or ask,
      if it offend thy love, which would
      always live in me.
Let me die to myself, that I may serve thee;
let me live to thee, who in thyself art the
true life. AMEN

Teresa of Avila
Spain
Sixteenth Century